ASK ME A QUESTION AND I'LL ANSWER

ASK ME A QUESTION AND I'LL ANSWER

DANIELLA NICHOLLS

Ask me and I'll answer....

*

How to use this book

Close your eyes and think of a question - open the book - run your finger along the page and when you feel like stopping, read the advice or message for you. You can ask as many questions as you like...

*

"We all make mistakes - you're only human, give yourself a break."

*

"Angels are helping and guiding you right now."

*

"Miracles from heaven are on the way"

*

"Write down what you like and dislike and then decide."

*

"Time is valuable, don't waste it."

*

"Make memories and enjoy."

*

"So what is your life worth? It's worthwhile."

*

"You're a fighter."

*

"Engage with people who lift you up and give you positive vibes."

*

"Someone close to you is pretending to be your friend - keep your eyes peeled."

*

"You will attract good friends."

*

"Jet set off somewhere new and enjoy."

*

"Invest in your well being."

*

"Live your best life and smile."

*

"Do not wait any longer, the time is now - you will be a success."

*

"If you encounter a few bumps in the road - don't worry, ride them out - success has your name on it."

*

"Invest in you"

*

"You can always sense when something is about to happen"

*

"You communicate well"

*

"Give yourself a chance to catch up."

*

"You'll be up to speed in no time."

*

"You are a boss."

*

"Look at someone with fresh eyes."

*

"You are perfect."

*

"You have a good heart."

*

"Make plans for the future."

*

"Your partner is being honest."

*

"Fear is just being human."

*

"Dance the night away and feel free."

*

"Meeting up with friends or a family member would be good for you right now."

*

"You are very intelligent."

*

"You have a pure and open heart."

*

"Your heart is always in the right place - you're just misunderstood."

*

"Meditate or do some yoga."

*

"Hit the gym hard - your body will thank you for it."

*

"You are a sweet person."

*

"You're like a bullet right now - unstoppable."

*

"Your soon to be life partner is coming sooner than you think."

*

"When you look good you feel good."

*

"Stop-breath-carry on."

*

"Try to stop overthinking it's making you anxious."

*

"You're anxious, take some deep breaths and try to meditate when you can."

*

"Don't let your health put you off living your dream."

*

"You will get better - give it some more time."

*

"This is an opportunity to grow - take it."

*

"Your life is now full of choices - take time to choose wisely."

*

""You inspire people."

*

"You have excellent judgement."

*

"Appreciate the people who have helped you through your journey."

*

"Sometimes in life you have to lose everything to gain it all back and more."

*

"Life is for living - the time is now."

*

"Value yourself and your family."

*

"You are a spiritual person."

*

"Taking time to meditate will make you feel good."

*

"It's time to be responsible."

*

"There is no time like the present - go for it."

*

"You're inspirational."

*

"Wait, the time is not right now, but that doesn't mean it won't be tomorrow or next week."

*

"Stand up for yourself."

*

"It's time to relax and unwind."

*

"Your life grows more relaxed and less reactive."

*

"Walk away - don't let people keep hurting your heart."

*

"You have strong likes and dislikes - choose and go for it."

*

"Stop the negativity and bring in the positive."

*

"Your comfort zone is becoming less important - the time is now."

*

"You don't need to follow the crowd to stand out, you already do."

*

"You may find you want to slow down and that's ok - take time out for yourself."

*

"You are a winner."

*

"If you feel it in your gut you know what to do next."

*

"If it doesn't work out - you have many days ahead to try and try again - you will make it."

*

"If social media is getting you down and making you feel insecure - stop looking at it."

*

"Perseverance is key right now."

*

"You have to understand that you can't please everyone."

*

"Go for it - you've thought about it long enough."

*

"The time is now."

*

"If they have to brag about it - then they're not really that good."

*

"When the opportunity arises don't wait any longer - go for it."

*

"Anything is possible - believe and it will happen."

*

"You are unique- enjoy it."

*

"Difficulties that have come your way will soon fizzle out - leaving you feeling ready for anything."

*

"Stop living in the past - open your eyes to a bright future."

*

"Just stop for a minute and enjoy the beauty of nature around you. It will do you the world of good."

*

"Take a hard look at your life and have gratitude for what you have."

*

"Anger does not solve anything - take time to understand and you will see what you were looking for."

*

"Just for today, put your phone away and have a stress free day."

*

"Try introducing organic foods into your diet - stay away from processed foods."

*

"Keep a sense of humour - it's ok to laugh and enjoy yourself."

*

"Life is far too short don't waste it."

*

"Use your common sense in this situation."

*

"Don't put undue pressure on yourself - you'll get there."

*

"You're on the correct pathway in life keep going."

*

"Something you have never dreamed of is about to happen to you - get ready to recieve."

*

"You are going through a stage of transformation for the better."

*

"Don't underestimate the hole your absence will leave - just think about that for a second."

*

"We all have something to offer in this world and so do you."

*

"Dont give up - keep going."

*

"You don't have to be the best to be successful."

*

"Remember when one door closes another one opens."

*

"Personal ambition is worth fighting for."

*

"Surround yourself with people whose eyes light up when they see yours."

*

"You can learn to be successful."

*

"Being kind to someone goes a long way."

*

"Smile life is good right now."

*

"Embrace the new change around you."

*

"Try to forgive others, we all make mistakes."

*

"It's time to set some new goals now."

*

"Write a life plan and try to stick closely to it."

*

"Read a book and get lost in it."

*

"Give someone near you a compliment and - will make their day."

*

"Treat your body with respect and fuel it with good nutrition."

*

"Try introducing more fruit into your diet - your body will thank you for it."

*

"It's time to add more vegetables into your diet and see the difference it makes."

*

"Stop repeating the same cycle - it's time to break it now."

*

"Be careful not to spiral out of control."

*

"You have an addictive personality."

*

"You are on another level compared to some people and that's where the problem lies."

*

"Staying humble is a great trait to have."

*

"Stop making the same old choices you always have - it's time for a change."

*

"It's time to put this relationship to bed once and for all and move on."

*

"You have made many mistakes but that doesn't mean you can't put it right now."

*

"You can always start over - you just need the courage to do so."

*

""The most beautiful people on this earth are not well known but you are one of them."

*

"Don't make the big mistake of comparing yourself to others - that leads to a downward spiral."

*

"Marriage is on the cards for you right now."

*

"Someone very special is preparing to propose to you."

*

"Stop spending all your time in your head - get out and do something."

*

"Stop being inaccessible to people."

*

"Blessings are coming your way right now - get ready to receive."

*

"There is a reason why that business opportunity fell through your fingers - because something bigger and better is coming your way."

*

"Watch the sunset and feel the comfort you get from it."

*

"You may come across as quiet but the truth is - you know more than most people because you take time to listen."

*

"You're due a long awaited shopping spree - enjoy."

*

"Just because you do not want to do anything right now- does not mean you are lazy. You are consciously deciding what step you are about to take."

*

"It may well be your fault but that doesn't mean you can't put it right."

*

"Having a job is great but you really need to work on yourself right now."

*

"You can make a fortune with this idea."

*

"There is greatness within you - you just need to seek it out."

*

"That person who has helped you behind the scenes - let them know how much you appreciate them."

*

"Don't forget where you came from and who paved the way or gave you the opportunity to do so."

*

"Giving to and supporting charity foundations is a noble act."

*

"You can make your own path in this life, you just have to believe you can do it."

*

""You're independent but take time to listen to someone giving you advice right now."

*

"A good decent human being will not put you down, as they are fulfilled enough themselves."

*

"You're dealing with something which is deep rooted - you will get through it."

*

"You don't need to carry on in a toxic relationship - the choice is yours."

*

"Make a different choice."

*

"You have turned a corner in your life and it feels good - keep going."

*

"Sometimes you have to stop doing things for others - because they do nothing in return for you."

*

"You can be naive at times, be careful who you trust."

*

"Betrayal hurts but you can come out of it fighting."

*

"It's not ok to let a cheater back into your life but sometimes they can change."

*

"Not everything you do needs to benefit you."

*

"Being so selfish is a ugly trait."

*

"Whatever you are thinking about right now - make it your destiny."

*

"You are powerful."

*

"Health is worth more than money, cars and gifts."

*

"Live like there is no tomorrow - no rules."

*

"As you think you become."

*

"Be patient with yourself."

*

"Great things are not achieved all at once - take one day at a time.

*

"A new day comes a new opportunity - take it."

*

"Your precious human being - take care of yourself."

*

"Feeling stressed out and anxious - meditate or take a bath with candle light and listen to soft music."

*

"Your relationship deserves another chance."

*

"You deserve to be happy - you know what to do."

*

"You're growing and changing but it's ok - go with it."

*

"Make it happen you can do this."

*

"Things are meant to be used, not people."

*

"It's time to stand on your own two feet - you've got this."

*

"You feel a strong spiritual connection with someone."

*

"It's your life - choose what you want to do with it."

*

"The spark between you and someone special is real."

*

"This won't be your only career - your more talented than you realise."

*

"You have a raw and natural talent - anything you put your mind to you can make it happen."

*

"If you have been thinking about doing something for over a year now. Stop thinking about it and make it happen."

*

"You feel the need to feel alive - take up a new sport or hobby."

*

"Bring fitness into your life and you will see the change you have been dreaming of."

*

"Take a break, you deserve it."

*

"Happiness comes from within."

*

"A holiday is needed right now."

*

"Take the leap of faith."

*

"No one can do things for you but you can make things happen."

*

"If you're not happy you need to do something about it."

*

"Do whatever makes you happy."

*

"Sometimes you have to make the choice to be happy."

*

"Make a wish - it will be coming true sooner than you think."

*

"Be patient, things are lining up for you."

*

"Your life is about to change for the better - get ready."

*

"When you are in nature it works wonders for your soul."

*

"You usually stay steady and steadfast when problems arise - this time will be no different - you will get through it."

*

"You need to start being kind to yourself - yes you deserve it."

*

"Making a few bad choices does not make you a terrible person. You can turn things around."

*

"Remember life is for living - what are you waiting for get out there."

*

"IF you believe this is the right choice to make then it is."

*

"You hate seeing loved ones upset - know you are trying very hard to make things better."

*

"Your health is important to you. Other people may not see that but you are doing your best to get fit. You should be proud of yourself - keep going."

*

"Your in a good place right now - enjoy it."

*

"You deserve unconditional love."

*

"You have worked so hard for so many years now - it's time to take a step back and chill. It's me time."

*

"You're feeling trapped right now - you have to make a change to feel good again."

*

"I hope you are ready for this, a new relationship is coming your way."

*

"An ex lover wants you back - choose wisely."

*

"You have longed and wished for this for so long - your significant other is about to enter your life - get ready."

*

"Know that you are important and worthy."

*

Your dreams are turning into an unbelievable reality right now - enjoy it."

*

"Your a real life angel - you have goodness running through you."

*

"You have spent many many hours, days and weeks looking after people - now it's your turn to look after yourself."

*

"You deserve the best."

*

"You are so loved - more than you could ever realise."

*

"In this situation there is no love lost - it's just an adjustment that's required."

*

"Choose wisely."

*

"Pick your arguments carefully - you don't need to win everytime."

*

"Your soul is yearning for peace and tranquility right now."

*

"You need to be realistic, it's impossible to be happy all the time."

*

"Time management is an issue for you right now - take time to master it effectively."

*

"Sometimes you're too honest for your own good - just remember to break it to them gently sometimes."

*

"Your development is crucial to your success dont let haters get in your way."

*

"Full hands on the throttle - go for it."

*

"Stop thinking so little of yourself - you know you are worthy."

*

"Don't worry about what the next person is doing right now - you do you."

*

"We are all on our separate journeys in this life."

*

"It can't be wrong if you're not hurting anyone and it makes you happy."

*

"Mediate right now to rejuvenate."

*

"We have this precious gift called life - make the most of it."

*

"You worry about just about anything - take time to relax and let the worries take care of themselves for a change."

*

"You have prayed for so long for a child and a child is coming your way, remember there are children out there, just wishing they could have parents like you both, Fostering and adoption are viable choices too."

*

"The love you knew to be pure and genuine has now gone to heaven, know that special heaven sent person, walks with you in your journey of life."

*

"Someone you love and cherish has departed to heaven - call out their name and they will come to you."

*

"People will tell you it's too complicated and put you off - but that is what they think or their experience. Your experience may not be the same, so go for it."

*

"We all feel lonely at some point in our lives but you can do something about it. Reach out to a friend, join the gym or join a hobby group."

*

"You have been feeling depressed due to past events. This cloud will be lifting away from you and you'll be feeling back to your old self soon."

*

"Yes, yes, yes go for it."

*

"You're much wiser than people think."

*

"Healthy mind, healthy body - look after yourself."

*

"What you have dreamt about is coming to fruition."

*

"You can always say no - if you feel it's not right."

*

"Don't feel pressured to do something you do not want to do."

*

"You have many choices - pick one."

*

"Communication is key in this relationship - take time to listen to each other without interruption."

*

"Your parents are proud of you - you need to know this."

*

"You deserve a break - go away somewhere beautiful."

*

"Tell someone you love them - they need to hear that right now."

*

"You do so much for your family but what about you? It's time to get pampered."

*

"Life is all about balance - we just have to get that right."

*

"We always wait for the right time to say or do something but in reality the time is always now. Don't wait a minute longer."

*

"This life is your journey and not anyone else's. Do what is in your best interest."

*

"You are feeling happy right now so anything is possible."

*

"It's ok to live your dreams and not your parents' dreams."

*

"Being helpful to someone right now means the world to them."

*

"You have had to make some difficult choices lately but know you have made the right ones."

*

"It's never too late to improve your job prospects - learn a new skill or enroll on a course."

*

"You're sensitive by nature but that's ok. Sometimes you need to let people know how they made you feel. Often they haven't a clue."

*

"Prepare yourself - a new journey is coming your way."

*

"The new beginning gets you excited and happy."

*

"Listen to your intuition and gut."

*

"Life Is about precious moments."

*

"Yes you are enough and don't let anyone tell you any different."

*

"It feels horrible when someone doesn't see your point of view, but don't worry - in time they surely will."

*

"It's difficult when your partner doesn't have your back - but don't worry you will soon realise you don't need them and you can do whatever you want by yourself."

*

"What's the worst they can say? don't let rejection put you off when it comes to relationships or jobs."

*

"Ask that special person you have liked so much on a date now."

*

"Don't let the doubt creep into your mind - you can do this."

*

"Don't let failure put you off your dreams - sometimes we just have to chase harder to catch them."

*

"Loving angels watch over you - you are in safe hands."

*

"Your spirit guides watch over you and help you through this journey called life."

*

"You're in that mindset now where you're going to show people just how talented you really are."

*

"Yes without a shadow of doubt you will be successful."

*

"Live your dreams."

*

"Do not look back - keep moving forward."

*

"The only time you can look back is to see exactly how far you have come."

*

"Put the kettle on, have a cuppa - everything will be ok."

*

"Just remember you are your own person."

*

"If you doubt something don't rule it out completely - it might be the right thing after all."

*

"You are a kind soul."

*

"You are loved and appreciated."

*

"You make a positive impact on everyone you meet."

*

"Don't question yourself - of course you can do this."

*

"You know the answer - you can most certainly achieve your goal."

*

"Reach for the stars and beyond."

*

"Don't wait for the change to happen - make moves to make the change."

*

"Don't doubt your abilities even though you find this tough."

*

"You have enough strength to ride out any storm that comes in your path."

*

"Go above and beyond your wildest dreams."

*

"You are a star."

*

"Have more self worth."

*

"ITs been such a long time coming but at last you are finally seeing the fruits of your labour flourish."

*

"It certainly is ok to ask for help - go get it."

*

"A new lover comes into your life in the next month."

*

"Try not to take yourself too seriously."

*

"It feels awesome to laugh and play."

*

"Take your partner on a date and rekindle that passion locked inside."

*

"You need to know the love for you will always be there - that will never change."

*

"If you have only got that one moment - enjoy it."

*

"Your happiness is a choice."

*

"If you carry on doing what you usually do, you will never see the change you are hoping for."

*

"If you make the change you will see a different result you were hoping for."

*

"Life is given to us to enjoy and experience new wild things."

*

"People want to be like you - so go set the trend."

*

"Your passion will shine through for everyone to see."

*

"This love will be kind."

*

"This love will be true."

*

"This love will not let you down."

*

"Forgive and move on."

*

"You deserve good love."

*

"You are the definition of love."

*

"You are beautiful."

*

"You are capable."

*

"You are capable but do you want it enough?"

*

"Time will tell if you were right."

*

"An opportunity has your name on it."

*

"You are blessed."

*

"You have the determination and skill to achieve anything."

*

"If in doubt, sleep on it to get clarity."

*

"If you think it, believe it, you can then most certainly do it."

*

"The grass can be greener on the other side."

*

"You need time and clarity to make this decision."

*

"The white feathers you see are from someone special in heaven."

*

"Don't worry too much this problem will resolve itself."

*

"Its ok to feel frightened - in time you'll become brave too."

*

"Your heart skips a beat for someone else."

*

"You have love for someone else."

*

"The love you have has grown and become stronger."

*

"You know it's ok to be different."

*

"Of course you don't fit in because you're unique."

*

"There is no love like your parents love."

*

"Love is in the air for you right now."

*

"You're going to meet someone so unique you'll fall head over heels in love before you know it."

*

"You lead from the heart."

*

"Don't let your health get out of control before you take it seriously."

*

"Incorporate vegetables in your diet."

*

"Incorporate more fruit in your diet."

*

"You've not been feeling yourself lately, if your symptoms persist seek medical help."

*

"You have a great business idea."

*

"No, not yet try again tomorrow."

*

"You will be good for each other."

*

"You will both bring out the best in each other."

*

"This kind of Jealousy is not healthy."

*

"You are in a great relationship."

*

"You feel it's the right time to leave this relationship - and it is."

*

"Experience new things."

*

"When was the last time you did anything for yourself."

*

"You are bright, intelligent with great attributes - who wouldn't like you."

*

"This job has got your name on it."

*

"If you are looking to put down on a property now is the time."

*

"Now is the perfect time to get away."

*

"That person you like so much just needs to know you exist."

*

"Make the first move."

*

"Someone special is looking down on you from heaven and is so proud of the person you have become."

*

"Never give up."

*

"Failure is no excuse you can do this."

*

"You need time to heal."

*

"You need time to grieve and that can take as long as you want."

*

"Your grieving give yourself a break."

*

"You're hurting right now - the pain will ease in time."

*

"You'll never be forgotten."

*

"Meet up with some friends - it's time to have fun."

*

"Better days are coming your way."

*

"It's time to make new friends."

*

"You're optimistic and that's a great quality to have."

*

"You fall in love easily - look after your heart."

*

"Your career means everything to you - don't forget to make time for yourself."

*

"Family members can be tricky to be around sometimes. If they don't want to know you - walk away.

*

"Give yourself time to come to terms with the situation."

*

"Someone has broken your heart - you will get over this, you just need more time."

*

"Someone in heaven is watching over you and loves to keep up to date with what you're doing."

*

"Keep positive."

*

"Your relationship had already come to an end - long before you made the decision to walk away."

*

"You feel something is missing in your life - figure it out and go for it."

*

"It is extremly hard to come back to someone who has hurt you so much - know that you are stronger than you think. You're ready for anything that comes your way."

*

"Your dreams are coming true now - when you see the rainbow that will confirm it."

*

"If you're desperate for a change in your life right now - then this is the perfect time to do it."

*

"Take time to sit in the sun and let those beautiful rays of sunshine stroke your skin - it will do you the world of good."

*

"Everyone enjoys being with you right now."

*

"You are a precious gift - don't let yourself go to waste."

*

"You're drawn to water right now - go to the beach and watch the waves go by, you'll feel yourself again soon."

*

""You don't do negative people and rightly so."

*

"Let people know if they want to vibe with you - then its positive vibes only."

*

"Keep staying positive."

*

"Stay uplifted, you are coming through the other side now."

*

"The abundance of wealth is coming your way - get ready to receive."

*

"You already know you're the brightest spark around, don't let anyone put out your fire."

*

"You are bright and a wonderful person."

*

"Your actions speak for yourself."

*

"If you don't like to go to a certain place - speak up now."

*

"Let your feelings be known - people can't read minds."

*

"You know exactly what to do in this situation - you're just looking for reassurance, you've now got it."

*

"Try not to waste your time with grudges - let it go."

*

"What you need to do right now is walk away and forget about this person."

*

"You wont meet anyone new if you don't close the door on the person who is in your life at the moment."

*

"Only you can put a stop to being used."

*

"What you want will work out for you right now."

*

"Give yourself a chance to catch up with this situation - it will be resolved."

*

"Your mum loves you so very much - hold on to that."

*

"Your dad loves you so very much - hold on to that."

*

"I know all you want right now is to be loved. That love you crave for will come your way."

*

"Wanting love from your fellow siblings and not receiving it can be tough - but in time the pain will lessen."

*

"I know you don't feel it in your heart but your family do love you."

*

"You have an untapped talent - look inside to see what it is."

*

"Your unique talent could make you very wealthy."

*

"You need to wake up - you can't let yourself be treated in this way. You deserve better."

*

"You need to understand that anyone would be grateful to have you as a boyfriend or girlfriend."

*

"At your job you are the boss."

*

"Everything about your job you hate. It's time to look for something different."

*

"Your maternal instincts are setting in - it's time."

*

"You know this isn't right - it's time to seek help now."

*

"You can preserve your eggs for future use or if you feel time is not on your side."

*

"You are doing your best at motherhood - keep going, you've got this."

*

"Being a mum can be really hard work and it's ok to question if you're doing a good job - that's normal."

*

"Rejection can be difficult to come to terms with but just know we all go through it at some point in our lives. You will get over it and bounce back."

*

"You're generous, kind, warm and loving - who wouldn't want you."

*

"Stop thinking about it now and take the plunge."

*

"Life is far too short to hide away - be social, you'll love it."

*

"Your life really does not need to be so complicated - declutter."

*

"It can be tough when friendships end - just know you will be ok."

*

"You are a beautiful person inside and a beautiful person outside."

*

"You would literally walk on hot coals for your family - you have a good soul."

*

"You don't feel appreciated at the moment - take time to tell someone how you're feeling."

*

"A change in career will bring you prosperity."

*

"You have the capability to make more money than you ever wanted."

*

"This very important purchase will go through for you."

*

"If you really want it, be prepared to work hard for it."

*

"It's your dream to provide exceptionally well for your family - keep going it will turn into a reality."

*

"Eat well and live well."

*

"It's ok to have your own friends and go out when you're in a relationship."

*

"You dream about being slim and fit - it's time to put some action into these thoughts - you can achieve this."

*

"Have a romantic meal with your loved one."

*

"Love is in the air for you right now."

*

"Your awful nightmare is just a bad dream - try not to read too much into it."

*

"Moving on can be really tough but know you have the strength to do it."

*

"Expect great things coming your way."

*

"You will be the success you so desperately want to be."

*

"Sometimes the best thing to do is apologise."

*

"Having high expectations is fine but can you fulfil someone else's expectations the same way?"

*

"There's never been a better time to do this - go."

*

"Stop worrying it will be ok."

*

"It's time to get your sexy back - work on yourself."

*

"What people think of you is not your business - go about your day and ignore them."

*

"Haters hate, ignore them and be your fabulous self."

*

"Stop putting doubt in your mind - you could take on the world if you only believed."

*

"The strength you're praying for is within you."

*

"You don't need to be afraid - Angels walk by your side."

*

"The only person who can make your dream happen is you."

*

"You enjoy preaching to others - right now you need to take your own advice."

*

"It's a long time coming - money is coming to you right now."

*

"Your kindness always gets your own way."

*

"Sometimes people can't feel the passion you have but that's ok."

*

"A new and exciting venture is coming your way."

*

"This relationship is really good for you - at last you feel you can be yourself."

*

"You don't feel safe and secure in this relationship - it's time to move on."

*

"Your cooking skills could bring you in a lot of money."

*

"There is no excuse for abuse - stay away from such people and seek help."

*

"If you feel like there's no way out - get help, it's out there - it will be the best thing you'll ever do."

*

"You're honest and trustworthy - you're a great catch."

*

"You both argue and wind each other up but just take a second and think how it made you feel - remember the other person may be feeling the same.

*

"Just because you argue doesn't mean there isn't love there."

*

"You're not in this relationship to be walked over and hurt all the time - get out and as far away as possible. You deserve happiness and peace."

*

"Being betrayed can feel like a knife in your heart - don't worry you will heal from this, and come back stronger."

*

"The more you think about it the more you will think yourself out of it. The time is now to go for it."

*

"You are needed right now - do not walk away just yet."

*

"Life throws us curve balls but we just have to navigate through them."

*

"Bide your time - your time is coming."

*

"Happiness has finally found you."

*

"A stable and lasting relationship is 50.50"

*

"A business you acquire will do exceptionally well."

*

"Working with children or adults comes naturally to you."

*

"Your passion lies with planet earth and you won't stop until you make it a better place."

*

"You love everything to do with law and order and would make a fantastic career choices for you."

*

"Religion means alot to you and would make a great career choice."

*

"You are extremely creative - use your skills and show them off to the world."

*

"Show business is your business."

*

"A career in modelling would come naturally to you."

*

"You know the feeling of wanting mum or dad never changes and has no age limit or time."

*

"You have a raw acting talent."

*

"You have the ability to be a great musician."

*

"Sport is your life."

*

"The sports profession would be a great opportunity for you right now."

*

"You're passionate about politics - make it a career move."

*

"Healthcare has your name on it."

*

"A career in agriculture would suit you."

*

"You can become more than what you are."

*

"Singing comes naturally to you - make it your career goal."

*

"You find anything to do with science fascinating, this can be a great career choice for you."

*

"You're obsessed with computers and a career in this field is meant to be."

*

"Your interest in beauty comes to you naturally - this would be a great career choice."

*

"Your interest in archaeology could be your career."

*

"A career in dentistry would suit you."

*

"A career in medicine would suit you."

*

"You have a real passion for space, make it your career choice."

*

"It's ok not to know your career choice - for now turn your hand to anything. It won't be long before you decide."

*

"You don't need to respond to someone trashing you, just walk away."

*

"You love and adore all animals and this could be a great career choice for you."

*

"Your life shouldn't be all work - you need to take time to relax and have fun."

*

"Guilt will only bring you down, try and let it go and start again."

*

"Everyday can be a new beginning."

*

"You dream of someone coming to rescue you but you know you can rescue yourself too."

*

"Make moves to improve your life."

*

"Your child is truly a star."

*

"Be grateful for your life - someone out there is praying to be in your shoes right now."

*

"Don't trust everyone you meet, be cautious."

*

"You are sensitive and articulate."

*

"Your new love interest is showing you real love."

*

"If you don't go for it now - someone else will."

*

"You're not just a dreamer, you visualise and make things happen."

*

"If someone does not have faith in you - have faith in yourself."

*

"If your partner can't support your dreams and aspirations - you need to ask yourself the question why."

*

"The best way to prove someone wrong - is to make it work."

*

"Aim high in life."

*

"You were born to do this."

*

"You are destined to be successful."

*

"A pet brings you healing right now."

*

"Your pet loves you as much as you love them."

*

"If your in a relationship or your living with family members - stop for a minute and just watch and see how hard they are trying to look after you #appreciate."

*

"Go for a walk and breathe new life into yourself - you'll feel better for it."

*

"Making mistakes is normal, just try to learn from them."

*

"Sometimes you feel you need to control every situation - it's ok you don't need to be in control all of the time."

*

"You can be anyone you want to be."

*

"You have a life that people can only imagine about - be grateful."

*

"You are a blessed soul."

*

"You need to remember you haven't had things handed to you on a plate like other people, you've busted a gut to be where you are."

*

"Your dreams and aspirations are important to you and they should be important to your partner too."

*

"You havent worked this hard for someone to tell you they won't factor in your dreams and aspirations."

*

"You're independent and proud."

*

"Love isn't being controlled by your partner."

*

"Your love life brings joy and happiness right now."

*

"Cling onto whatever gets you through this difficult situation - You will get through this."

*

"Climate change is a real concern for you right now - we can all help to make a change."

*

"Your life is about to make a 360 for the better."

*

"It's ok to move out and spread your wings."

*

"That special someone you have been wanting for will come into your life now."

*

"It's ok to put yourself first sometimes."

*

"Disappointment can be hard to deal with but you will come through it."

*

"It's time to stop running away and face the problems your running from."

*

"You feel happy and free right now, enjoy it."

*

"It's hard being an adult sometimes."

*

"You do have a handle on this problem and everything will work out for the better."

*

"Moving on doesn't mean we forget - we still have them close in our hearts and minds."

*

"Your relationship is under some strain right now but it is strong enough to weather any storm that comes in your way."

*

"Don't keep those feelings bottled up - write down how you feel or talk to someone - you will feel better for it."

*

"The world of arts is your life - make this your career."

*

"You could be rich and famous."

*

"Your feeling frustrated right now - start a fitness program and feel the frustration wash away."

*

"If you want the abundance you deserve - take time to meditate on it and visualise."

*

"It's important for you to stay fit and healthy for the future."

*

"Keep yourself active and challenge yourself mentally to keep you in good stead throughout life."

*

"Make a list of what qualities you have - you'll be surprised what you have to offer someone."

*

"Your judgement is good - trust yourself."

*

"Your perception is amazing - use it."

*

"You don't need to put restrictions on yourself."

*

"Don't make excuses for yourself if you want to achieve."

*

"Being honest in a relationship keeps it alive and well - if you want to kill it keep lying."

*

"Its ok to be a bit possessive sometimes just don't make it a regular thing."

*

"Sometimes we have no choice but to experience painful situations."

*

"You have a secret admirer."

*

"You can be bold and brave."

*

"It's not the be all and end all if you lose that match they'll be another chance to win."

*

"Be gentle with yourself - it's not that you're forgetful, you have so much on your mind right now."

*

"They say there's no such thing as Mr right but he's coming your way very soon."

*

"It's ok to want to be on your own sometimes."

*

"They say there's no such thing as Mrs right but she's on her way to you soon."

*

"You are not a mistake - you are a gift from god."

*

"Sometimes life can be unkind but happier days are on their way."

*

"It can be tough in your environment but hang in there - it will be coming to an end soon."

*

"Happiness will find you again when you least expect it."

*

"Trust me you've got this."

*

"You are awesome in every way."

*

"It's your life to make your own choices."

*

"Convince them you know best."

*

"Don't let jealousy ruin your relationship."

*

"We come in different shapes and sizes - it's normal."

*

"The gym, fitness program, and nutritionist can all help with your fitness goals."

*

"You're worrying about a body issue - we all have something we don't like about ourselves. If you feel like your concerns are getting out of hand - seek professional advice."

*

"The world is yours for the taking."

*

"You're a beautiful shining star."

*

"You are a fantastic role model and people look up to you."

*

"You always deserve respect."

*

"Walk away happy knowing you tried your best to work things out."

*

"It's ok to feel sad sometimes - if you feel you're being consumed by it, seek professional help."

*

"You deserve happiness in your life."

*

"Sometimes it's good to be quiet in a conversation - you'll be surprised at what you will learn."

*

"You don't need to be loud to get noticed - you get noticed anyway."

*

"You're a real head turner and you know it."

*

"People admire you."

*

"Don't let jealous people put you off what you want to do."

*

"You are a smart person."

*

"You fantasie in your head and that's ok."

*

"You are normal."

*

"A friend you know needs you right now."

*

"You are a great friend - just make sure your friends are doing the same for you."

*

"Spending some time with your family members will be good for you."

*

"You are the queen bee right now."

*

"It's important you keep the line of communication open right now."

*

"We all say bad things in a heated argument sometimes but you can bounce back from this even stronger."

*

"It's ok to want so much more from life."

*

"You expect the world and why not you deserve it."

*

"Only time will tell who your real friends are. You do have good friends too."

*

"Don't put up with bad behaviour."

*

"You're a good decent human being, you deserve nothing but the best from life."

*

"Being cut throat with your tongue isn't you."

*

"In your head you need clarity right now."

*

"Putting pen to paper and writing how you feel will help you right now."

*

"Your dream is coming true."

*

"Your health concerns are bothering you - get checked out for peace of mind."

*

"Who said you're old - you're never too old to try or do something new."

*

"Having a date night will bring back the spark you need in this relationship."

*

"A real friend will uplift you and not put you down and make you feel sad."

*

"It's ok to live for today as long as you're being responsible."

*

"You can do anything you want to - you just need to put the hard graft in."

*

"Sometimes it feels like people don't want the best for you but you are old enough to decide what is right and wrong."

*

"When you're older you'll realise your parents just wanted the best for you."

*

Dedication

"This book is dedicated to Ann, Sarah, Daniel
and to my parents who i have boundless love for."

Daniella Nicholls is a writer and author. A spiritual person who enjoys the world of meditation and yoga.

www.ingramcontent.com/pod-product-compliance
Lightning Source LLC
Chambersburg PA
CBHW071857160426

43209CB00005B/1089